Greater Than a Tourist Dubai United Arab Emirates

50 Travel Tips from a Local

>TOURIST

Wajiha S. Khan

Lock Haven, PA

All rights reserved.

ISBN: 9781521559109

>TOURIST

DEDICATION

This book is dedicated to all those who are fiercely loyal to my aimless, meaningless wandering.
All one of you.

BOOK DESCRIPTION

Are you excited about planning your next trip? Do you want to try something new while traveling? Would you like some guidance from a local? If you answered yes to any of these questions, then this book is just for you.

>Tourist, UAE by Wajiha S. Khan offers the inside scoop on Dubai. Most travel books tell you how to travel like a tourist. Although there's nothing wrong with that, as a part of the Greater than a Tourist series this book will give you tips and a bunch of ideas from someone who lives at your next travel destination.

In these pages you'll discover local advice that will help you throughout your stay. Greater than a tourist is a series of travel books written by locals.

Travel like a local. Get the inside scope. Slow down, stay in one place, take your time, get to know the people and the culture of a place. Try some things off the beaten path with guidance. Patronize local business and vendors when you travel. Be willing to try something new and have the travel experience of a lifetime.

By the time you finish this book, you will be excited to travel to your next destination. Ten cents of each book purchased is donated to teaching and learning.

CONTENTS

CONTENTS

Author Bio

How To Use This Book

WELCOME TO >TOURIST

Introduction

1. Know Your Seasons

2. Pick The Perfect Lodging

3. Stay Adapted

4. Learn Some Rad Phrases

5. Get Acquainted With Local Transport

6. Grocery Like A Pro

7. Meet Your New Friend: Arab Cuisine

8. Meet Its Cousin: Nonresident Arab Cuisine

9. Have A Drink Or Two

10. Pose For The Burj

11. Check Out The Palm Islands

12. Stroll Around The Marina Walk

13. Take A Walk Down Memory Lane

14. Take A Literal Walk In The Park

15. Get Tanning

16. Attempt To Summit The Dubai Mall

17. Explore The Indoor Marine Scene

18. Meet The Dubai Dino

19. Treat The Kids To A City Their Size

20. Synchronize With The Dancing Fountains

21. Picnic In Dubai's Snow

22. Bash Dunes, Not People

23. Go Camel-Riding

24. Befriend Your Friendly Neighborhood Dolphins

25. Admire Islamic Architecture

26. Connect With Nature at Mushrif Park

27. Say Hi To Some Furry Friends

28. Say Hi To Some Fluttery Friends

30. Chill By The Creek

31. Have Dinner At A Dhow Cruise

32. Get Water-Sporty

33. Level Up Your Surf Game

34. Dare To Take The 100-Foot-Plunge

35. Hit The Beach And The Park At The Same Time

36. Take A Long Drive

37. Hang With Superheroes

38. Watch A Movie Under The Stars

39. Capture The Metropolitan Skyline At Night

40. Celebrate The Arts

41. Explore The Open Market

42. Go Pearl Diving

43. Have A Traditional Lunch Or Dinner

44. Go Faux-Skydiving

45. Go Actual Skydiving

46. Ride A Hot Air Balloon

47. Have An Educative Shopping Experience

48. Cash In On All The Sales

49. Don't Need Dollar Bills To Have Fun Tonight

50. Honorable Mentions

> **TOURIST**

> **TOURIST**

> **TOURIST**

Author Bio

Wajiha is a resident of Dubai, a part time high school student, and a full time maverick insisting she can write. She loves to study, form unsavory opinions, and dream insanely big.

She loves to travel across the city, sometimes on foot, because love makes a person slightly unreasonable.

Wajiha moved to Dubai at four years of age, then spent all of her phases from the formative to the annoying ones living there. This caused the city to strongly rub off on her.

Whether in the form of warmly welcoming and befriending people, or in the form of finding it ecstatic when an elevator full of people as different as night and day smile at one another, the charm of Dubai has diffused into Wajiha's core and she feels no shame in flaunting it.

Wajiha's affair with her city also makes her enjoy the finer things in life, such as the occasional gold-plated Mercedes, a stroll within the largest mall in the world, and the view of the tallest building on the planet from everywhere in the city. It is, in fact, the little things in life that count.

Through its appreciation of all that is different, Dubai taught the author to admire even what others may consider eccentric, completing the process of claiming her as its very own.

How To Use This Book

This book was written by someone who has lived in an area for over three months. The author has made the best suggestions based on their own experiences in the area. Please check that these places are still available before traveling to the area. Get ready to enjoy your next trip.

WELCOME TO >TOURIST

Introduction

Located in a country called the United Arab Emirates (U.A.E.), Dubai is a modern and glorious Middle-Eastern city. It is rich in heritage, rich in grandeur, and rich in making its residents and visitors feel very, well, rich.

If you are a nervous traveller or are generally wary of new places, rest assured, because according to the World Economic Forum as of 2017, the UAE is the second safest country in the world.

We all know Dubai for its extravagance: it hosts the tallest building in the world (Burj Khalifa), a mall that could be a city on its own (The Dubai Mall), and one of the most expensive hotels in existence (Burj Al Arab).

What you should also know about the city is that it is home to some of the most warm and wonderful people on the planet. Its big-hearted nationals look for excuses to make their guests feel at home, which is why millions of wonderful people, like yourself, visit Dubai every year.

If the seven wonders of the world amaze you, Dubai's got all the modern swagger to blow you away with a peer into the future, as opposed to the nostalgia of the unseen past.

So whether you intend to have the most exciting, bucket-list-toppling vacation imaginable, or hope to kick back and chill like you've never chilled before, Dubai has something or the other in store for you that'll make you glad you came!

1. *Know Your Seasons*

First off, let's certify that Dubai is (metaphorically) the coolest city to have ever existed within a desert, if not in the whole world. But being a desert nevertheless, its weather is limited to either raging summers or breezy winters. Keeping this in mind, try to book your vacation between the months of November to March. That way, you'll be able to balance indoor activities with outdoor ones. In case you're unable to do so, it's still alright, because Dubai's indoor activities exist in abundance and are lots of fun. You will, however, be limited to them, because a few special outdoor events only take place in the cooler season, such as the annual 'Global Village'.

2. Pick The Perfect Lodging

Whether you're ready to splurge, or are looking to stay soft on the pocket, Dubai has an array of hotels ready to impress. Though there are many other offerings too, you may be able to find one tailored to your suiting in one of the following popular areas:

- Downtown Dubai

- Mina Seyahi

- Al Barsha

- Creek, Deira

- Dubai Airport, Deira

3. Stay Adapted

While the U.A.E is a very progressive country, it prides itself in its rich Islamic heritage. This means certain guidelines must always be kept in mind: alcohol consumption is limited to certain designations and is generally prohibited in public. Pork is rare, but is offered in many hotels and supermarkets. Decent dressing must always be maintained; swimwear is allowed only in pools and most beaches. Overt displays of affection are strictly not allowed, and serious racial/religious harassment is punishable by hefty fines.

Ladies are given high importance in the U.A.E. Dubai Metro holds dedicated 'Women and Children' compartments, and lady-driven taxis exclusive to families and women are also available for those who would prefer to use them. It is not customary for men and women to greet each other by shaking hands in the U.A.E.

Remember that if you're going to be exposed to the outdoors for long, a good way to beat the heat in Dubai is by staying hydrated and engaging in water-related activities. Wear light and airy clothing, minimize the amount of things you're carrying around, as well as your exposure to sunshine. Wear sunscreen and a wrist band to wipe away perspiration. Go heavy on the deodorant and maybe supplement it with talcum powder if you're super conscious. Keep this gear on you at all times: hats, caps, sunglasses, and water bottles.

4. Learn Some Rad Phrases

The official language of the U.A.E is Arabic but English is generally spoken and understood. Some common phrases of the Arabic language are:

"Salaam-u-alaikum" – Peace be upon you. This is a way of saying hello.

"Wa-alaykum-as-Salam" – Peace be upon you too. This is the appropriate response to "Salaam-u-alaikum".

"Marhaba" – Welcome.

"Na'am" – Yes.

"La'a" – No.

"Kayf Halak?" – How are you?

"Shukran" – Thank you.

"A'fwan" – You're welcome.

"Ma'a Salamah" – Depart with peace. This is a way of saying goodbye.

"Maa hadha?" – What is this?

"Ayna/Limadha?" – Where/Why?

"Sabah el Khair" – Good morning.

"Massah el Khair" – Good evening.

"A'asef" – Sorry.

5. Get Acquainted With Local Transport

Local transport in Dubai is available in four forms:

- Taxi – for when you really have to get around and don't mind spending.

- Dubai Metro – for when you want to get to a landmark connected to the metro line, cut through traffic, and enjoy a solid view of the city on the go.

- Dubai Tram – for when you want to navigate around the Jumeirah and Dubai Marina area.

- Bus – for when you absolutely crave an adventure, or have more time than money to spare on travel.

I personally recommend buying a 'Nol' card – these are reloadable at gas and metro stations, and can be bought from the latter. They enable easy check-in and check-out on public transport.

6. Grocery Like A Pro

Not all days can be days spent eating out, so buy some groceries and make the stay more personal. Locals get great deals and sales from:

- 'Carrefour' outlets
  (Found in the 'City Centre' chain of malls; Carrefour Express stores are also found commonly among most neighborhoods buildings.)

- Cooperative stores
  (E.g. 'Union Cooperative', 'Emirates Cooperative', etc. These are large supermarkets containing imported products, usually but not exclusively from within the Middle East, which establish cooperation between the gulf region. One big outlet of these stores is often found in the middle of several separate localities.)

- e-Supermarkets
  (Apps and websites that provide an electronic alternative to physical grocery shopping. They may have great sales and offers sometimes, but beware of shipping costs.)

7. Meet Your New Friend: Arab Cuisine

All perks aside, you've got to admit, one of the best parts of travel is eating all the best food a new place has to offer. Since Dubai's past involved lots of 'being a harsh desert', the typical diet would contain very few vegetables. Therefore, some traditional must-haves in the U.A.E are:

- Mandi – meat of chicken or lamb cooked in a 'taboon'(i.e. special kind of oven involving a hole in the ground covered by clay, fueled by wood and charcoal) coupled with rice; heavenly when paired with a side of tomato sauce.

- Shawarma – grilled meat shavings wrapped in flatbread along with tahini, hummus, fries and pickle. This is the Arab wrap.

- Falafel – deep-fried spheres made from chick peas, fava beans, or both. Kind of like a hipster savory doughnut.

- Manaqeesh – flatbread with cheese, or ground meat, or a herb called za'tar, in whichever combination you choose. The Arabic alternative to Neapolitan pizza.

- Mixed grill – various assortment of grilled and barbecued meat served with side of hummus, flatbread, tahini, eggplant dip. Will give the American barbecue a run for its money.

- Biryani – although not a local dish, it has become part of the tradition here due to a high number of sub-continental expats. Made of rice, meat and spices. Sounds like Mandi, tastes like a whole other society!

Note: Anywhere you decide to try these dishes from, if you tell them you're vegetarian, they will definitely cater to you accordingly. Dubai is nice that way.

8. Meet Its Cousin: Nonresident Arab Cuisine

Talking about food is one thing, but when talking Dubai food? There are bound to be outrageous variations - and I'm here to enlist them for you:

- French toast with Date jam at Creekside Café.

- Cardamom and dates crème brûlée at Creekside Café. (Tastes as wicked as it sounds.)

- Camel Burger at Local House Restaurant. (Yes, that genuinely means burger made of camel meat.)

- Camel milkshake at Al Majlis Café . (Pretty exclusive and not half bad. Genuinely made of camel milk, which scientifically has more nutrition than cow's milk. Win-win?)

Honorable shoutout to 'American Shawarma' which is an Arabic dish with a foreign twist. It contains an excessive amount of fries, more kinds of meat (e.g. 'turkey bacon', which is absolutely fabulous), a side of cool ranch sauce and the glorious taste of liberty.

9. Have A Drink Or Two

We've already established that alcohol is not warmly received out in public, in Dubai. That doesn't mean there aren't other zesty alternatives to keep you going! We're not savages. Here are some local specialties:

- Laban: A buttermilk drink that's known to quench thirst in the desert. Comes in sweet or savory offerings. Personal recommendation: have the sweet stuff. Best served cold.

- Tamar Handi: Essentially a tamarind sorbet, this drink is sweet and sour and best served chilled.

- Jellab: The closest 'halal' will get to wine; this is a blend of grapes and rose water, topped with pine nuts and raisins.

- Arabic coffee (Kahwa): Like espresso, but aromatic. Ditch the usual latte on this one; one tiny traditional cup packs quite a punch. Served hot.

- Karak chai: An English breakfast tea variant, only much stronger and often far less fanciful. A genuine drink, 10/10 recommend. Served piping hot!

10. Pose For The Burj

If I haven't already mentioned the two 'Burjs' of Dubai multiple times, I'll do it now. Once in Dubai, it's mandatory to click that selfie with Burj Khalifa whether you do it from the airplane, from afar, or in-house.

The tower is decked with exclusive cafes and restaurants, and a gallery called 'At The Top' from where you can see far and wide. So while you're having at it with the selfies, have high tea to go with it.

Later on when you decide to hit the beach, strike a pose twice as fancy with Burj Al Arab - one of the most luxurious hotels in the world. Also one of the most iconic symbols of Dubai.

>TOURIST

"I am not the same, having seen the moon shine on the other side of the world." – Mary Anne Radmacher

>TOURIST

11. Check Out The Palm Islands

There are three specific islands in Dubai that are shaped like palm-trees lying across the ocean, because why not? Those are:

- Palm Jumeirah

- Palm Deira

- Palm Jebel Ali

The oldest one is Palm Jumeirah, host of the astounding Atlantis Hotel, based on – you guessed it – the city of Atlantis, lost under the sea. The amount of awe-striking activities on offer here cannot be justified in one paragraph, and so have earned their own 'tips' further in the book.

(Tip Numbers 24, 34, 35.)

12. Stroll Around The Marina Walk

If you're coming to Dubai, you might be interested in seeing where 'posh' peaks. Luckily, that's a purpose this beachfront promenade serves.

The walk down the pathway is long, but that is a good thing – once you've spent the whole day here, you'll get to see the golden view transcend into a glimmering, concrete night.

Speaking of which, nightlife is avid in Dubai Marina; complete with top-notch bars and electric nightclubs. If you're big on those things, this is one of the coolest places in Dubai for you.

13. Take A Walk Down Memory Lane

For those of you who are still interested in the nature of humanity: Firstly, you're precious. Secondly, Dubai's Heritage and Diving Villages are genuinely perfect for you.

Buried within one of the city's oldest localities and only a 9-minute drive away from Dubai Museum and the preserved palace of Sheikh Saeed Al Maktoum, this is Dubai's historic hub. You'll find everything you need to know about how Dubai used to be before oil 'happened', right here.

If you like stories, you'll love this place; it speaks for itself in telling the rich, coming-of-age tale of Dubai.

14. Take A Literal Walk In The Park

Sure Dubai is a scintillating desert, but apart from the occasional blazing weather, that statement is used mostly for effect. You'll find a myriad of green belts and parks here. Some great options are:

Zabeel Park – divided by the trance-inducing Sheikh Zayed Road, connected via a pedestrian bridge. I profess that said bridge offers one of the most gorgeous sights of Dubai. The park also features standalone attractions such as 'Dubai Garden Glow' and 'Dubai Dinosaur Park' (no real dinosaurs).

Creek Park – Starring: The Dubai Dolphinarium, edutainment center 'Children's City', and boat rides across Dubai's Creek.

Pond Parks – several of these parks are located across Dubai. With a uniform pond-centric design, all of these are fantastic, but Al Barsha Pond Park meets the cut for the least crowded experience even on weekends.

*More parks in Tips 26, 36.

15. Get Tanning

When in Dubai, do as the weather allows: grab some tanning lotion, hit the beach, and get your tan on! Just remember that topless sunbathing is not a thing here. Having said that, the nicest beaches for a peaceful sun-basking are:

- Kite Beach: Crystal-blue waters, yellow sand, the occasional holiday maker kite-surfing and having a good laugh. These are a few fun attributes of Kite beach – apart from the fabulous view of Burj Al Arab, of course.

- Burj Beach: Speaking of which, walking along Kite beach closer to the Burj will lead you to the area called 'Burj Beach'. There are volleyball nets here, and visitors also enjoy playing football – a sport tattooed on the heart of every U.A.E national.

- Open Beach: Located on Jumeirah Street, this neat beach offers one of the most spectacular views of Burj Khalifa and Dubai's urban metropolis by the sea.

*Beach-parks have been skipped as they qualify for Tip 36.

16. Attempt To Summit The Dubai Mall

Ah yes, the world's largest mall (by area) covering 5.9 million square feet of land, hosting more than 1200 stores and outlets. Basically, if you can't find something here, it just doesn't exist.

Dubai Mall is located right next to Burj Khalifa in the ritzy area of Downtown Dubai. If you want to be at the core of the city's swank, be here.

The mall has its own stop on the Dubai Metro link, but be warned; the (air conditioned) bridge from the metro station to the mall has a distance of about a thousand meters so it's quite a walk!

The sheer number of attractions in this mall are so atrocious, they demanded separate 'tips'.

(Tip Numbers 17, 18, 19 and 20-ish).

17. Explore The Indoor Marine Scene

Getting on the topic of The Dubai Mall, once there, you'll likely come across the Dubai Aquarium. It's kind of hard to miss, what with being one of the world's largest indoor aquariums. Hosting more than 140 species of sea-creatures, (you can say that's a lot of...spe-seas) the aquarium even offers the options of either watching the marine beings from afar, or going through an acrylic tunnel and feeling closer to being a mermaid.

18. Meet The Dubai Dino

In case you're a fan of time travel, just visit 'The Souk' wing of Dubai Mall. Laced with a traditional vibe, it's home to the fully intact fossil of a brontodiplodocus. So, you know, be that close to 150-million-years-ago. No extra charge. No charge *at all*.

19. Treat The Kids To A City Their Size

In case your kids are anything like all the kids I have ever taken to Dubai Mall, the 'Candylicious' store opposite Dubai Aquarium would have caught their attention, and soon you would've got yourself a sugar-powered-monster crisis. Don't worry, because there are ways to 'train the dragon' within the mall itself.

Take them to the video game-themed arcade called 'Sega Republic' where they can emulate their inner Sonic the Hedgehog; take them ice skating at Dubai Ice Rink; and if all else fails, take them to Kidzania.

Kidzania is a model city, all child-sized, where the young ones can get degrees, a driver's license, jobs, a credit card, and other such things.

Everything is in partnership with real-life organizations such as HSBC, Dubai Driving Institute, McDonald's, etc. The experience feels so real, you'll start getting nostalgic about things the kids haven't even accomplished yet!

20. Synchronize With The Dancing Fountains

Not in the mood to discover or get bedazzled? Not a problem! Right outside the Dubai Mall are the majestic dancing fountains of Dubai. Portraying a water channel flowing downtown, blended with music and soothing watery wondrousness, you'll find tranquility in just sitting by the fountains and watching the day age.

>TOURIST

"I wandered everywhere, through cities and countries wide. And everywhere I went, the world was on my side."

— *Roman Payne, Rooftop Soliloquy*

>TOURIST

21. Picnic In Dubai's Snow

We've come to an understanding that a whole lot of Dubai's awesomeness is held inside of its malls. If you're wondering how far this goes, well, suffice it to say that Dubai has a literal snow park inside of Mall of the Emirates.

Going by the name of 'Ski Dubai', this icy hangout spot features an 85-meter-high slope down which you can ski or snowboard, then cable-car your way back up. At its base, you have the emulation of a tiny snow village where you can build snowmen, have snowball fights, and basically live in an alternate reality where there are winter towns in the middle of a desert.

Even Disney's 'Frozen' has got nothing on that.

Disney's 'Frozen' does, however, have a thematic influence on the snow park. Maybe when ticket time's up, you'll know exactly how to remind your kids to 'let it go'.

Dubai Metro does stop at Mall of the Emirates, making it a very convenient commute.

22. Bash Dunes, Not People

One of the most signature 'Dubai' things to do are activities in the desert, such as falconeering, or a desert safari, or camping, or a barbecue picnic.

During your stay here, you should try to do at least one or two of these things, because nothing says "I just had the best of the Middle East!" like a selfie with gorgeous sands in the background.

You can book an organized trip with an excursion agency which will usually include a high-speed ride in a four-wheel-drive, a resting area for refreshments, and an arrangement for dinner.

23. Go Camel-Riding

As one could say: "When in the desert, sail its ship." (Get it? Get it?)

You can get a camel ride with an excursion group for a tour in the desert, or you can go camel-riding at Jumeirah Beach if you'd rather have the experience sea-side. If you're feeling even fancier, Creek Park hosts camel rides too, so you can include that on the to-do list for your trip there.

If you're the kind of person who loves animals and want to really connect with this rare-ish majestic creature, plan a trip to Al Sahra Equestrian Center. You get to meet camels in their natural habitat, hear about their history, and even get to taste their milk!

24. Befriend Your Friendly Neighborhood Dolphins

For some reason, Dubai has no shortage of creatures for its spectators to behold and ravish. So if you're intrigued by the general pleasantness of dolphins and how friendly they are, not only can you see their super-smartness at the Dubai Dolphinarium in Creek Park, but can also swim with them and befriend them at Dolphin Bay in Atlantis Hotel.

It's just another one of those spectacular things we have here that doesn't need to be questioned, really.

25. Admire Islamic Architecture

Having a relationship with a place is a lot like having a relationship with a person; if you really want to get to know it personally, you should keep an open heart about its religious values. Following that idea, make a visit to Jumeirah mosque. Open to followers of all religions, the mosque gives you a chance to see how a place of worship remains a place of worship no matter where in the world it lies, or what religion it's aimed at.

Because there are always ways to connect with humanity for those who're interested in finding them.

26. Connect With Nature at Mushrif Park

Speaking of connections; if you're looking for one with nature, then Mushrif Central Park is going to be just the place for you.

Since it is located in a very relaxed, upscale community full of people who like to chill and make the most of life, you'll be right at home chilling alongside them. Like the people who visit it, the park has two sides: one is a raw, untouched, natural desert habitat; the other is landscaped, refined, and holds lots of different attractions.

The gigantic park comes complete with a swimming pool, equestrian club and a 500-seat theater, in case nature isn't the only thing you're compelled to connect with.

27. Say Hi To Some Furry Friends

Another lovely place to connect with nature in Dubai is its polite little zoo. You'll find more than a hundred different species of creatures here, although some may not be as 'furry' as they will be 'feathery.'

Entrance is outrageously inexpensive too, with a cost of 2 dirham per person, and children under 2 years of age going free. So while the zoo may entertain its monkeys with peanuts, it kind of appeals to everyone else with them too.

If you find yourself tired and hungry at the end of the trip, there's the classy 'Mercato Mall' close by, for refreshments as well as a very well-deserved look around.

28. Say Hi To Some Fluttery Friends

Remember how we came to the realization earlier about how Dubai is so nonchalant about giving its visitors the chance to get up-close with exotic creatures? Here's another one of those extravaganzas: an indoor butterfly garden.

Dubai's 'Butterfly Garden' has nine covered domes; home to more than 15,000 butterflies which, if you're counting, is actually a lot of butterflies. With numbers that high, it's very likely you'll find perfect lighting at the same time as the perfect pair of wings, so keep a camera at the ready.

The best part about this indoor insect haven is that it's open all your round. So you get a butterfly picture, and I get a butterfly picture, and everyone who visits any time of the year gets a butterfly picture!

29. Marvel At The Miracle Garden

Right next to the Butterfly Garden, you have the dumbfounding and surreal landscape of Dubai's Miracle Garden. Sculpted entirely out of flowers in the most splashy way imaginable, walking through this place is like taking a stroll through Alice's Wonderland!

From heart-shaped walkways to life-size cottages, to an Emirates aircraft; everything is modeled with an enormous array of gorgeous, colorful blooms.

Because of course Dubai found a way to be extravagant via nature.

Unlike the Butterfly Garden though, the entire scenery is set in the outdoors, so you'll only be able to visit it in the winter. This is exactly why it neighbors the 'Butterfly Garden', which is absolutely splendid in its own right, and is a fair make-up deal if you do have to settle.

30. Chill By The Creek

Basically, the Creek is to Dubai what Central Park is to Manhattan; almost all of the city lies around it. You can get a wildly different array of stuff done there, depending on which side of the creek you're on. Here's a list of things at the ready:

- You can visit Dubai Festival City, best known for its IKEA but also generally an outstanding indoor shopping promenade.

- You can head to the iconic 'Dubai Creek Golf and Yacht Club'; a leisurely waterfront landmark of Dubai which can be considered actual chilling headquarters.

- There's the 'Ras Al Khor Wildlife Sanctuary', where thousands of birds migrate to and then lounge around in, so you could hang out with them if you wanted to.

- There is also the aforementioned Creek Park, where you can do general outdoor park stuff.

A lot of the creek's surroundings have already been mentioned even outside of this section. It's all in the logistics; you'll understand as soon as you grab a map.

>TOURIST

"Every one of a hundred thousand cities around the world had its own special sunset and it was worth going there, just once, if only to see the sun go down."

- Ryu Murakami

>TOURIST

31. Have Dinner At A Dhow Cruise

You'd think luxury cruise dinners are an exclusive experience, but Dubai has a way of making even that more special as well as more accessible at the same time.

Enter the Dhow cruise: a classic Arabic boat tweaked on the inside to serve as an impressive, traditional Arabic restaurant. The following choices offer the finest of experiences:

- Dhow Cruise Dubai Marina

- Rustar Floating Restaurant

- Dhow Cruise Creek

- Zomorrodah Dhow Cruise

32. Get Water-Sporty

For how many times I've gone over Dubai's heat, its summer and its desert climate, I now present to you its finest compensation: a bunch of things you can do to make the most of these things.

Firstly, hit the beaches mentioned in previous tips, on most of which you can go parasailing, wake-boarding, paddle-boarding and kite-surfing. The most readily available activity is jet skiing, and it's perfect for the summer-haven feeling that Dubai generally perpetuates.

Moving away from beaches to man-made structures, check out these two water parks for water slides and a lot of other aquatic attractions:

- 'Aquaventure' at Atlantis Hotel

- 'Wild Wadi' in Jumeirah

If you find these options too basic,, you can also go scuba diving at 'The Dive Center' in the Dubai International Marine Club.

And then comes the boss level: 'Shark encounter' at the Dubai Aquarium in Dubai Mall. In full diving gear, you'll be accompanied by an instructor who will feed the sharks right next to you while you gape at them in awe, because yes, this experience is definitely awesome.

33. Level Up Your Surf Game

We're all hit hard that 2015 did not bring us hover-boards; instead we're stuck with Segways that barely even look half as cool.

At least there's the hydraulic alternative though – 'flyboarding.'

A 'flyboard' is basically like a water-powered hover-board; you get to haul yourself into the air high above the waves and maybe flip around and do cool acrobatic stunts on it. Dubai is rated one of the 7 most exciting places in the world to have this experience in, so have a stab at it while you can.

Go wild; it's as far as we've come as a species. For now.

34. Dare To Take The 100-Foot-Plunge

Dubai's generally the kind of place that encourages a person's wild side. For example, if you're a thrill seeker, Wild Wadi's 'Jumeirah Sceirah' attraction is aimed specifically at you, since it's one of the world's top ten most exciting water slides.

With a 105-foot-drop that has you zooming at the speed of about 80 km/h, this is basically one of the most extreme childhood fantasies that could ever come true. The altitude makes for quite a sight too, so maybe enjoy the view on your way down?

35. Hit The Beach And The Park At The Same Time

Ever wanted to be in two places at once? Well the good news is, you've got the option to be at a beach and a park at the same time. Here's the bad news though: they've got a word for that, and it only counts as one place - a beach park.

Two of the best beach parks in Dubai are listed below. They both qualify as amazing standalone parks or beaches too, but the hybrid makes them super special. They are:

- Mamzar Beach Park: One of the most splendid experiences you and your family can have in Dubai. Since it overlooks the neighboring city (Sharjah), you get to enjoy a beach park as well as a Dubai-Sharjah border. You can also rent a chalet at the beach and make a proper day out of your visit.

- Jumeirah Beach Park: Another wonderful spot for the family. Ideal for barbecues, picnics, and a general fun day out. Closer to mainstream Dubai, so there's more of Burj Khalifa and Burj Al Arab in sight.

36. Take A Long Drive

U.A.E's infrastructure is pretty solid, and let's be honest, its total land area is pretty small. You know what that does mean, though? The most convenient road trip you could ever imagine.

If you have an International Driver's License, make a Google search of the car rental that fits your wallet best, get a ride, and get going.. You can travel south to the capital city of Abu Dhabi, or to the North where lie the sweet states of Sharjah, Ajman, Umm al Quwain, Ras Al Khaimah and ultimately, the mountainous city of Fujairah.

(Cities double as states here; it's a tiny country. Even the longest drive will take a maximum of just 3 hours.)

If you've ever dreamed of driving a Rolls Royce or a Ferrari or any other exotic car, you know, like a normal person, you can snag a great deal on those too!

Whether you have an International Driver's License or not, Dubai believes in giving you a great car experience. Hence most rent-a-cars offer valet services as well. So grab a backpack, keep your favorite music on you, and hit the road!

37. Hang With Superheroes

If someone at Disney Land went: "Guys! Guys! Imagine if everything was exactly this much fun, but with *zombies*, *dinosaurs* and *superheroes*;" they would actually be talking about Dubai's 'IMG World of Adventures'.

To be fair, that means you can hang out with more than just (Marvel) superheroes here. There are Jurassic feels to be felt in the 'Lost Valley' attraction, comical kinds of fun to be had in Cartoon Network's own wing, and of course, there ought to be chills and screams dedicated to the nerve-wrecking 'Haunted Hotel'.

A standard ticket, which includes access to all of these zones, costs AED 245. Children under 1.20 meters go for AED 225, and the even tinier ones below the height of 1.05 meters go free.

38. Watch A Movie Under The Stars

Humanity can agree that out of all things ever, the night sky is one of the absolute best – if you want to make it feel even more magical than it already is, grab a special someone and take them for a movie screening under the stars. (In case you're traveling by yourself: you're special, you're someone. You're your own special someone! And for half the price too. Go you!)

You can visit the rooftop cinema at The Galleria Mall - Jumeirah, where you can enjoy one of the latest movies under the bare sky. The stars won't be the only thing twinkling, because this theater faces the dazzling scenery of Dubai's metropolis in all its raw, nocturnal majesty. Tickets can be booked via VOX cinemas' app or website.

For a literal price-less experience, visit the 'Pyramid Rooftop Gardens' in Wafi Mall on a Sunday at 8:30 PM. There are beans bags to chill on and classic flicks to feast on. Screenings change every Sunday, as does your mood every time you sit through one.

39. Capture The Metropolitan Skyline At Night

Whether through a walking bridge, or through the window of a fine-dining restaurant, you must take a moment to breathe in Dubai's stunning night skyline.

It's breathtaking. It's spectacular. It's like a carpet of stars in a room where the ceiling is the rest of the universe. It's simply beautiful.

Some of the best places to catch this magnificent sight are:

- Level 43 Lounge, D.I.F.C. Gate Building

- Marina Walk, Dubai Marina

- Footbridge, Zabeel Park

- Walking Bridge: Emirates Towers Metro Station, Financial Center Metro Station, Burj Khalifa/Dubai Mall Metro Station

- 'At the Top' – Burj Khalifa (costs AED 125, book in advance.)

- Taj Hotel – Treehouse, Burj Khalifa Boulevard (drinks start at AED 80.)

40. Celebrate The Arts

For how much Dubai loves fine living, you'd imagine it would obviously hold some very decent art galleries. If you are one of those with an acquired taste and a refined palate, or if you generally like silence and staring at beautiful things, do visit:

- Art Sawa – 08, Gate Village, D.I.F.C.

- The Empty Quarter – 02, Gate Village, D.I.F.C.

- Art Space Gallery – 03, Gate Village, D.I.F.C.

- RIRA Gallery – 02, Gate Village, D.I.F.C.

These galleries are buried within 'Dubai International Financial Center', a wondrous part of Dubai not many people seek out to venture. With a vibe so European painted with so much tranquility, you'll be surprised by the mesmerizing tone of this very lush wonderland.

>TOURIST

"Two roads diverged in a wood and I; I took the one less traveled by." – Robert Frost

\>TOURIST

41. Explore The Open Market

There's just something really satisfying about trading out the blandness of paper currency in exchange for a fascinating new thing. All one really needs is an excuse, and an abundance of options to be spoiled with. Luckily, Dubai's always going to be there to validate your need to spend; so if you feel like putting your wallet on a diet and getting it acquainted with fresh air, check out:

- ARTE, The Makers Market – Times Square Center/Mercato Mall/Oasis Mall.
  More of an exhibition of handmade goods; this is an artist's place to shine. Held throughout the winter months on various weekdays, it features the likes of intricate jewelry, hand-caved woodwork, aromatic candles, and all kinds of things made with love.

- Reform Night Market – The Lakes
  These theme-based markets are a fit for all the birds of the night (weeknights, to be specific) who'd fancy bagging a bunch of novelties such as organic clothing, intricate beachwear, vintage goodies, and the likes. Massages and manicures are on offer, so don't hesitate in making a proper night out of it.

- Farmers' Market On The Terrace – Bay Avenue, Business Bay.
  Held on Friday mornings, farmers here sell their best produce along with freshly baked goods, aromatic herbs, the sweetest honey of the region as well as handmade jams. This sort of thing really has 'morning people' making sense.

- Ripe Market – various locations and days throughout winter.
  Hosting all of the various products mentioned above in one huge space alongside al fresco dining, the Ripe Market is a free size option that won't let anybody down!

42. Go Pearl Diving

Back in the 1800's, the good people of the U.A.E earned major money by trading the authentic pearls found in their waters with the rest of the world. Today, this exclusive experience is available for anyone who wishes to have it, with several generations worth of tips and guidance at the ready.

Plan a trip to go pearl diving with an instructor; many diving tours can be found online, and one notable option is offered at Jumeirah, where you will be accompanied by an esteemed third-generation pearl diver. You'll be dressed in traditional pearl-diving attire, schooled on the Arabian waters and how to adapt to them, and most importantly, you'll get to keep any pearls you find.

It's literally a gem of an experience.

43. Have A Traditional Lunch Or Dinner

Having a traditional meal is not just about the cuisine you're having, but also about the style in which you're having it. For example, in the U.A.E, the traditional way of dining is on a floor setting. You sit along the spread of eatery on a carpeted and cushioned floor, while the big dish containing the main course sits in the middle and everybody eats out of it. This denotes a way of sharing; a way of telling the people you dine with that you love them. It brings all the people on the 'dinner table' together, and that's basically what lies at the core of Arabic values.

If you ask me, it's what makes the people of U.A.E such fabulous hosts.

44. Go Faux-Skydiving

Ever been fascinated by the idea of flight, but not the idea of plummeting towards the ground at the speed of 200 km/h? Well, don't worry about that last part anymore, because 'iFly Dubai' has found just the way to emulate the experience of skydiving at (kind of) ground level.

Here's how it works: two gigantic fans with a total of 800 horsepower are housed on either side of a 10-meter-high acrylic tube, and you are suspended in the middle via science. This replicates the part of skydiving where the diver is at terminal velocity, so you're floating and flying, but not actually moving in any direction.

The attraction is located inside Mirdif City Center. You are given instructional training as well as safety gear on site, and the experience costs AED 195 per person.

45. Go Actual Skydiving

If you're more of an adrenaline junky and want to feel like a true bird soaring over a very real landscape in the actual sky, 'Skydive Dubai' is definitely for you.

Offering a vast variety of options ranging from solo, first-time dives to formation diving for the experienced, you get the guidance of some of the best ever skydivers under some of the highest safety standard regulations in the world.

You get to choose between an urban dive over Palm Jumeirah, or a thrilling desert drop at the 'Desert Campus'. Prices all vary according to which program suits you, so visit their website for detailed planning.

If you're ever going to go skydiving, might as well do it over one of the coolest skylines in the world. After all, you're likely to remember it forever!

46. Ride A Hot Air Balloon

If you're going to have ultimate experiences on your vacation, a hot air balloon ride over the Arabian desert alongside a falcon while witnessing an Arabian Oryx in its natural habitat is about as ultimate as it gets. While the experience comes with the price tag to go with it, it also comes bundled with a five-star detour to a private desert reserve, as well as a special bedouin camp where a gourmet breakfast is on offer; featuring the likes of caviar, hand-cut smoked salmon, etc.

Check out 'Balloon Adventures Emirates' for this particular experience, as those guys are the most experienced in their field.

47. Have An Educative Shopping Experience

Dubai's options for indulgences are borderline insane, but they don't have to be entirely full of guilt. If you want to get a learning experience out of the absolute delight that shopping is, check out 'Ibn Batuta Mall'.

The theme of the mall is 'The adventures of Ibn Batuta,' who was a 14th century explorer. The guy road-tripped to places like Persia, China, India and Andalusia (Spain) despite living in a time when traveling didn't mean tapping a button to purchase a plane ticket.

Each court of the mall is designed in the manner of the regions he explored; artifacts and bits of information about his experience, as well as that era of history, are scattered throughout the mall so you can walk through his life in the most next-generation way possible.

Even if you're not looking to shop, this mall is a fascinating trip for the sake of its 'explorer' vibe; its huge, its design is more meaningful than that of others (see: *there is a literal life size elephant model in the 'India' court*) and it's packed with all the perks of modern society. The mall does not get as crowded as other malls either, since it is located in the slightly distant 'suburb' of Jebel Ali.

48. Cash In On All The Sales

Like the gift that keeps on giving, Dubai's chain of sales follow each other one after one, like dominos. Be it for Christmas, or Eid, or a change in season, or vacation season, or just because why not; there's a form of promotion right around the corner at any given point. The deals you can get are jaw-dropping, such as flat 50% off, buy-one-get-one-free deals, bundles that would otherwise cost more than double the price, etc.

To see this phenomenon in its prime, visit Dubai in 'Dubai Shopping Festival' season, which happens every year and lasts about 40 days. Every single mall or retail shop in the city takes part, which subsequently forces neighboring cities to join in. The whole place becomes one big shopping "WHOA!"

If you're a tech person, you absolutely must check out the annual 'GITEX Shopper' - a huge event featuring the latest developments in robotics and computer technology, which also features mega sales on electronics. When GITEX takes place, all of Dubai puts promotions on technology in its honor.

49. Don't Need Dollar Bills To Have Fun Tonight

We love cheap thrills!

No but seriously, it's true. Coming to a city full of exotic and elite influence does not mean you have to splurge like a royal to get the full experience. Here are a wallet-watcher's words of advice:

- Groupon and Cobone are your friends. You can get mind-blowing discounts and deal vouchers from them for an insane amount of experiences, activities and even products.

- Some of the yummiest food comes out of the least showy bistros. A casual meal of shawarma and chai won't cost you more than 10 dirham, if you find the right kind of café.

- When in doubt, get a McDonald's 1-dirham-cone.

- When the weather is pleasant, walking in Dubai as a mode of transport is easier than you'd imagine. It really isn't a ginormous city, and it's extremely safe too. I personally do it all the time.

- Visit 'Day to Day' outlets; these offer a wide array of very inexpensive products, ranging from souvenirs to stationary to clothing to kitchen tools, etc.

50. Honorable Mentions

For all the times I've emphasized on Dubai's size, here's the silver lining: its neighboring states (cities) are really close by, and also really awesome. Here's a bunch of stuff you should do there, if you do intend to check them out:

- Visit Al Majaz Waterfront in Sharjah for a gorgeous show of dancing fountains complemented by palm trees and a full-fledged park. Enjoy a breezy brunch while you're at it.

- Visit Al Qasba in Sharjah for an eventful lunch/dinner where you can get a ride in 'The Eye of Sharjah' and saunter through Al Maraya Art Gallery.

- Visit Ferrari World in Abu Dhabi for one speedster of a day; play interactive games, check out Ferrari 'museum' which holds different models of the car throughout the years, and perhaps get a ride on the world's fastest roller coaster. This place is basically Enzo Ferrari's version of Willy Wonka's chocolate factory!

- Speaking of speed, if you're a Formula One fan, I don't see how you can come to the U.A.E and not visit the Marina Circuit in Yas Island, Abu Dhabi. You can drive sports cars, take racing lessons, or watch different speedy events here.

- For the more culturally inclined, there's Abu Dhabi's 'Sheikh Zayed Mosque' – the mosque that is considered U.A.E's key site of worship. Adorned with beautiful architecture of Mughal, Moorish and Moroccan influence, you'll love this mosque if you deeply appreciate different customs.

Remember to live your experience to the fullest and have fun. Spread love, find peace – I hope to see you around!

\>TOURIST

> TOURIST

Please read other Greater than a Tourist Books.

Join the >Tourist Mailing List :
http://eepurl.com/cxspyf

Facebook:
https://www.facebook.com/GreaterThanATourist

Pinterest:
http://pinterest.com/GreaterThanATourist

Instagram:
http://Instagram.com/GreaterThanATourist

>TOURIST

> TOURIST
Greater than a Tourist

Please leave your honest review of this book on Amazon and Goodreads. Thank you.

> TOURIST

Greater than a Tourist

You can find Greater Than a Tourist books on Amazon.

Printed in Great Britain
by Amazon

24955067R00057